MY THREE LEAF CLOVER

Aditi Goel

BookLeaf Publishing

India | USA | UK

MY THREE LEAF CLOVER © 2024 Aditi Goel

All rights reserved.

No part of this publication may be reproduced, stored in a retrieval system, or transmitted, in any form or by any means, electronic, mechanical, photocopying, recording or otherwise, without the prior written permission of the presenters.

Aditi Goel asserts the moral right to be identified as the author of this work.

Presentation by *BookLeaf Publishing*

Web: www.bookleafpub.com

E-mail: info@bookleafpub.com

ISBN: 9789363316386

First edition 2024

*This book is dedicated to- My family and
Atreya.*

PREFACE

The purest form of friendship, the feeling of warm embrace
everything comes together, even darkness makes its place.
Possessiveness grows, turning my heart cold;
everything disappears, and cruelty takes hold.

NEVER LETTING THEM GO AWAY

Sitting in a circle surrounded by memories of
frowns and follies,
we shared the audacity to laugh at each other's
tragedies.
My friends are complicated, yet so simple;
our minds in perfect harmony, our conversations
ever so nimble.

We form the three-leaf clover, I am never letting
them leave.
I finally found someone who loves me enough to
believe.
I will hold them close in the sunniest of hopeful
days,

and in the times when all of us are drowning in
despair.

The players of the building blocks of my life,
they had become.
Balancing a weakened soul with all the patience
they can fathom.
They are the sunset that caused a fleeting
moment of solace,
and the sunrise that forced me to en-garde with a
smiling face.

The days we recall, like four friends about to bid
adieu.
While all but me are moving out for growth that
was quite due.
We sit and share the dismal days of the past
since those were the trauma-building days of the
amassed.

A harrowing memory of when a fight broke out;
Kabir's birthday it was, celebrations were
exuberant and profound!
Everyone dressed up and looked beautiful in
black and white;
drunk promises of separating were proclaimed
with dizzying moral heights.

During the days of shared speeches and clinking
glasses of wine,
we promised to stay close, never leave the other
person's side.
So, like the stem of the clover, I have decided to
stay;
holding my lucky leaves close, never letting
them go away.

HOW DARE THEY?

Did you, my closest three
know that you set my soul free?
Years ago, there was one who left me to wonder;
left me in despair, did I make a blunder?

I begged and cried, fell on that friend's feet;
they wanted to make me feel inferior and meek.
They left me, HOW DARE THEY?
Well sooner or later, they did pay.

"My friends, my treacherous allies,
our affinity is strong, yet full of beautiful lies.
However we cry, we laugh together with
blood-red eyes
but your betrayal of leaving me alone was a
ghastly surprise."

Many left my side, making me delusional.
People call me ill, but am I really that illusional?
"You three made me believe I can live without
fear
and breathe in with intrepidity because you three
are always near."

My colleagues laugh at what I always say,
I recite the humour Naina delivered the previous
day.
The clothes that Kiara finely selects and picks
up,
after Kabir, it became my confident getup.

"For you three are the reason why I succeed.
To keep you close, is my sole act of greed.
Try escaping my love, my warmth that always
grows over
because I am the stem in this three-leaf clover."

STITCHED DISGUISE

"Kabir, can we have a few moments
for me to scream my bottled-up sentiments?"
I held his hand and took him upstairs,
it was my time to discuss our past affairs.

With each step, the staircase played music;
the ever-abominable creek made him a sceptic.
While he tried slipping away, I held him and
said,
"Calm down. Take a deep breath instead."

We walk inside and I lock the room
and double lock the door by sticking a broom.
I turned around to look at my friend
who sat, leaning against the board of the bed.

"I look at you and always feel,

this act of mine is a vile ordeal.
Although you said you would leave the city,
you still asked me to come along, all in pity."

Why was he pitiful, why the façade?
Was I just the afflicted one from the quad?
"You crave love, you are desperate for
attention",
an excuse it was, they made it my intention.

"Please don't hate me, I know I have sinned
but your acts only made me chagrined.
Despite the humiliation, I did stand by.
I could not defy the promise; only comply.

Our friendship will be sustained forever
because we are the three-leaf clover!
My mistake is gruesome, I apologize.
I stitched a permanent smile, the perfect
disguise."

PENCIL

"My social anxiety makes me detestable;
plenty have called me 'unforgettable'.
Out of thousands, only you accepted me.
With you around, my face lights up with glee.

The first day of school, when I was nine
where none of my friends were truly mine.
Mrs. Chatterjee made me sit next to you,
I knew you would be the first of my crew.

Our initial conversation was about the parrot
who I so ruthlessly wanted to strangle to death.
You thought I was gawking with curiosity,
but, its murder was a reflection of my concealed
monstrosity.

I looked at the teacher when she asked,

having no pencil was a shame to be masked.
You see, my parents were nary truly available,
and their crimes will never be bailable.

They disregarded me, and did not even care!
Always bickered with each other on what was
'fair'.
This was the time, I was sad, and my only way
out
was to sit in my room to bawl and pout.

You understood me, you knew something was
wrong.
You knew I was scared, so you played along.
You told the teacher that the pencil belonged to
me,
it had fallen and I was unable to see.

You saved me then, you save me now,
you are my trunk and I, your bough.
Despite you gone, our friendship won't be over
because Kabir, you are the first leaf of my
clover."

MOON THAT SWOONED

Kabir and I get back, sit on the table
where Naina was sitting next to a bowl and a
ladle.
I handed it to her and said,
"Remember? You promised to keep us fed!"

Flashing back to a story so pure and gold
which I will cherish when I am grey and old.
Where time was frozen, and also fast-moving,
we sat and drank in a serene setting.

Laughter was shared, and with teary eyes of
humour,

we then drove drunk on the mountains on a
scooter.
Under the sky filled with a thousand twinkling
stars,
we sat and overcame our past scars.

After an hour of being each other's pillow,
after reaching a good point of mellow,
we drive back to the camps where we sat
and witnessed the conclusion of a lover's spat.

Under the mountains, the stars and the moon,
Kabir was the only man who made Kiara swoon.
The beauty of white mountains with fresh snow;
the beautiful valleys made a natural echo.

This one memory, I recall with wonder;
the influence of love which people are under.
Kiara is the one—Kabir's devoted lover,
the pure-hearted one in this three-leaf clover.

SORRY EYES

"Kiara, my friend and my sister indeed,
can we go to the kitchen, I feel dizzied?
Make me the lemonade, the cure I require
and talk to me in the words of satire."

Wherever Kiara walked, I walked beside her.
She makes my homesickness a blur.
Kiara is the embodiment of my older dead sister,
she was the warm blanket to my chilly winter.

We entered the kitchen, but she knocked over a
knife.
Why does she have the most frightened look of
her life?

Why is she scared, she is my family!
The only one who could ever give me amnesty.

I lean forward to whisper in her ear,
but she fell back out of fear.
I wasn't going to hurt her anymore;
just an apology to be delivered for the sins I
bore.

So I took her hand and looked into her eyes,
the depth of her sorry eyes made me realize
her thoughts about me could not be any lower.
I cannot tell her that I hurt my three-leaf clover.

CRYSTAL MODEL

"You are the first person I confide in,
Be it an emotion or the slight pinch of a pin.
My family's warmth, you always give;
you became my ideal home, not one where I
used to live."

Kiara knows everything about my life
from the dead sister to the constant strife.
"The only motive behind any achievement of
mine
Is to celebrate with you over a glass of wine."

"My heart felt heavy when you decided to leave.

I thought all your love was a vain attempt to
deceive,
But then you got me something surreal;
the encapsulation of our friendship in a
peripheral.

You saw me shiver, you saw me cry,
You saw me looking for ways to try;
try to stop you all from going away,
my sole motive was to make you stay.

So you, with sheer love and affection
bought me the finest gift from the selection.
It was a crystal model that showed you cared,
it was the bottle of the first poison we shared."

"How dare you expect me to be selfless,
to let go of love so precious?
You are my three-leaf clover, please listen?
My intentions are no longer hidden."

TEDDY BEAR

"Anyways, I think we should leave,
clearly all of you just misconceive."
With the warmth of my love, I hold;
like her body, her smile was also cold.

Wasn't the smile a bit brighter before?
The kind that reflected happiness' core?
However, you all smile, nothing beats the best
Naina's smile is what got me impressed.

It was a fine Sunday at the arcade
where not any game was left unplayed.
We went to encash the tickets we had won,
a whimsey choice to be made- a teddy or a gun.

Naina looked at the teddy bear and then away.

The pink ball of fur was staring back from the
display.
I pointed at the toy and she jumped,
my arm was her outlet where she thumped.

This was when she stole what was mine
Naina stealing my peace was a clear sign!

Nobody could outshine Naina's breathtaking
smile,
Like the blue waters surrounding a lush green
isle.

I fell in love for the first time in my life,
the intention is to make Naina my beautiful wife.
"Congratulations, my three-leaf clover, my
saviour,
your wait for me to have a partner is finally
over."

SLICED, STUFFED AND STITCHED

"Naina, my beautiful friend I deeply love,
for you are as gracious as a dove.
Loving you would be a lifetime of glory;
we will sing aloud our story."

I sat for hours, articulating my love for her;
everything other than thread and wool was a
blur.
I sliced, stuffed and stitched, I repeated;
it was a simple way to keep us completed.

Don't get me wrong, it was equally agonizing!
It was like the pain of you three patronizing.

Call it revenge, but it is a way for you to stay,
also for me to not feel like an aimless stray.

Like a hippie, I'd always carelessly wander
from misery, I'd start escaping like an
absconder;
listening to our song, the music we loved the
most,
the first theme of every single clink of toast.

'For when I was lost and found by none,
My friends made me feel like I have won.'
Who couldn't relate to the song, so true,
I also had friends who helped me make it
through.

My three-leaf clover, now you are free.
I have now fixed the last of you three.
You are not leaving, this is for sure,
For I have control over, but you have no cure.

MUSHROOMS

With great dread, I face the wrath of love
As I believe, there is no feeling even farther
above.
It is frustrating, it makes you malevolent,
But the overall gesture is overwhelmingly
benevolent.

Looking at Kabir and Kiara, so shamelessly
smitten;
innocent eyes like that of a widely-eyed kitten.
They breathed each other, they were never apart
Two of them were now sharing one single heart.

I wished for such love, but never found it
anywhere;
When one fine day, Naina came out of nowhere.

Entering my life like a magician someone hired,
Helped make me love my life, and I always got
inspired.

For her smile, I would kill a thousand men to
please
Every single day, with a bouquet fall to my
knees.
Having someone to love, is the one true purpose
of mine;
Being loved by someone is a feeling quite
divine.

"I saved from mine, I know you love
mushrooms."
Like that, she filled all the vacuums with love in
volumes.
Segregated them from the slices of pizza she ate.
Unknowingly, she sent me an intangible,
permanent bait.

I held Naina's hand and took her aside in the
corner
Asked her to come with me, why was her walk
saunter?
My three-leaf clover, why are you all scared?
Wasn't I the only one who selflessly and
endlessly cared?

SATIN PIECE OF CLOTHING

Caring was never a part of my nature,
Never had I seen any in the love chamber.
My parents never conventionally loved me. You
see,
They would be befuddled by the present me.

"It was you, Naina, who made me believe.
Love is something that you don't need to
achieve!
It is something that develops from within
Makes you want to become holy but also sin."

I held her hand like a satin cloth that was
soothing.

My dear Naina was also like this exquisite piece
of clothing.
The touch of classy, she portrayed so graciously
Never was there an intent to present
ostentatiously.

With beauty, she came with love in infinite
bundles;
she held your hand while passing the toughest of
hurdles.
So selflessly and naturally, she cured every
injury or illness,
she was the medicine to everyone's toughest
mental sickness.

"The day Kabir and Kiara went on a date, on
Valentine's Day,
It was just me and you during the sunset on a
Saturday.
We looked at each other, I knew there were
sparks indeed.
My mouth was quiet because your eyes I had to
read.

You looked at me when I cut my finger while
slicing the chicken,
covered the wound, and that got me
love-stricken.
Nobody ever cared for me whenever I came
home bleeding,

I would sleep alone; in the dark and loudly
weeping."

I know you're about to cry, the sensitive one of
us three.
Emotionally intelligent you are, you set your
soul free.
My three-leaf clover, please convince her to be
mine, I tried;
Every ask of mine she has always denied.

DESPERATE ATTEMPT

Naina is the peace to all my past misery,
her being in my life is now very necessary.
If she is not the reason why my past keeps me
awake
Then all of this, what I have done, is a big
mistake.

I don't make mistakes, this plan was flawless
I can't be the one who is awless!
"My three-leaf clover, I know you will
understand why,
This was the only desperate effort that was left
to try.

You are the only three who stayed despite
everything,
You brought me up from rock bottom where I
was nothing.
Now I am a person, a man with a purpose in my
life,
To keep you both with me and make Naina my
wife."

I had only one wife when Prachi asked me to be
hers;
It was a goofy game we played as
kindergarteners.
All fun and cute it was, but only till the time I
was betrayed;
Prachi held someone else's hand, and I was the
one who got played.

Years later, when I was a child about the age of
seven,
Samir, my friend, was around the age of eleven.
Like a sibling he was to me, I respected him
plenty,
but he beat me up for every issue, be it serious
or petty.

Finally, things improved, I can now make a true
friend,

Naina taught me, she is one on whom I could
blindly depend.
Naina, my love, thank you for changing my
luck,
she kept me grounded, not run recklessly amok.

I pick Naina up, to give her a treat for her
contribution,
like I did give Prachi and Samir their fair share
of retribution.
I picked her up, and placed her stomach on my
shoulder,
It felt chilly; her body had become colder.

THREE IMPORTANT QUESTIONS

My stomach was screaming while grumbling,
When I heard the noise of someone tumbling.
Naina and I walked down to find ourselves our friend
Who was fallen in the room, without a mend.

I put Naina on the table, opposite where I sat,
Sprinted towards the area where Kabir's body was flat.
Picked him up and placed him on his seat,
The dining table was full, it was finally time to eat.

I serve small portions to my smiling clover,
Their mouths need to be empty to answer;
Answer the questions that were eating me up
inside,
An honest correction to every time they ever
lied.

What should I ask first, I need to think,
Let me first fix myself a fat whiskey drink.
Whose betrayal should I bring up first?
How about the betrayal that was the worst?
"Kabir, why do you want me to stay away?
Why do you victimize yourself as my prey?
Why did you want to shift to another city,
work the same job there, is it because of me?"

"Kiara, you are irreplaceable, I hope you know.
Why did you have to stoop so low?
While saying you love me and will always be
there,
Where were you when I wanted to share?"

"Naina, why do you always reject me?
Why is my love still hopelessly deeper than the
sea?
Let us set everything aside, and I have one
question,
Will you say yes, and cure my rapidly increasing
anticipation?"

I am going to ask these questions every single
day,
They now know that I am never letting them go
away.
The last desperate attempt it was, and it was
successful,
To keep them with me forever, I need the
needful.

LEAVING TRACES BEHIND

They are now staying back, within proximity so close,
this is a joyous occasion, why is the setting morose?
To go through the abhorrent transgression every single day;
a new memory should be dwelled into, like the one at the café.

It was pelting, like the sky was crying at the divine hour,
where my friends and I were far from being dour.
The coffee was warm, bitter and loaded with froth,

Pastries were aesthetically placed on a plate
above a cloth.

The theme of the parlour was to let loose for
some time,
focus on relaxing a little, in an atmosphere
soothingly sublime.

That is when the waiter came to the table with a
note and the bill,
ours would be the first message to the café, we'd
start from nil.

Wondering what to write, we wrote something
humble,
'Officially the solution to your stomach's
grumble'.
The owner then came to us, asked us for the
note,
Clicked the smiling three-leaf clover to pin it to
on board.

The first memorabilia, the first tangible proof of
friendship,
proof of the result of endless gut-wrenching
hardship.
I had friends, I had a family, I had people I could
take everywhere.
We can mimic the groups I see on the street,
going about here and there.

That is when it struck me, to leave our mark at
important places.
Placed a three-leaf clover wherever we went, I
wanted to leave our traces.
I need to prove to everyone I knew, I know and
will know,
Not to pity me, because now I have friends and
not a single foe.

SORRY, KABIR.

The pencil, the one that made me devoted,
Kabir saved me and that made me indebted.
"You deserve to know the truth; it is only fair.
My pleasing blessing is your gruesome
nightmare."

People take any chance they get to discuss my
friend,
It gives me a chance to praise him, I never want
it to end.
However, they wilfully neglect one of his
biggest flaws,

Many ugly fights were instigated, where he was
the cause.

Kabir's magic is a façade of decency for
everyone around,
make them his friends and then pull them to the
ground.
The trick to the friendship he manipulates is to
endlessly give,
he was taught every nicety of the world, but
never to forgive.

"I apologized, I begged, and I stood at your gate
for hours.
Can we please resuscitate the amity that was
ours?
Yes, I cancelled the flight tickets to your escape
destination,
But you also left me cold and alone out of
agitation!"

Why did he lean forward, why did he have such
rage?
Why did he think that our house was nothing but
a cage?
The lost and helpless should not have sprinted
towards me,
My reflexes are sharp; so, I just set his soul free.

The pencil saved me once, it was going to save
me again;
but all you did was crib, whine, scream and
complain.
Not of friendship, but it was now a symbol used
to euphemize;
who knew, the same pencil would be the cause
of your demise!

You bled out on my hands, you stared directly
into my eyes,
I had started hallucinating blood-red-coloured
gloomy skies.
It then occurred to me; that you are not going
anywhere!
It was my time to be creative, and not despair.

I did just that, I picked you up and took you to
our house,
and cut open an innocent animal, the
experimentation was on the mouse.
I mastered the technique; it was not time to cut
and remove.
My friend had to be stuffed properly, I needed to
preapprove.

I cleaned up everything and gutted you very
neatly;

My acts were to keep you close; the intention
not beastly.
You were the first of the three-leaf clover to be
the skin
of the filling of a teddy bear, now handsome and
thin.

SORRY, KIARA.

My deceased sister used to come in my dreams,
Each one of them had antipode themes.
Like the stripes on a zebra, they never matched,
those dreams kept my dead sister and me
attached.

The day Kiara entered my life, I realized
she was the reflection of my sister who I so
dearly idolized.
The same eyes, the same smile, the same
kindness,

the way to portray everything is okay, to hide the
weakness.

I loved sharing with my sister, she was always
attentive,
Her care was precious, very gentle and purely
redemptive.
One fine day when I started to miss her, my
body was jittery,
I called Kiara to my house, to feel the only love
at parity.

I just wanted a hug, a shoulder to put my head
on and cry,
But she brought up a fact that I wretchedly tried
to deny.
During the much-needed hug which was nothing
short of the remedy,
My anger did not give me a second to even be in
jeopardy.

The glass model she bought me of the first
poison we shared,
During her visit, sat so elegantly right behind her
head.
While she hugged me, she lingered for a minute
or two,
Decided to invite her demise by mentioning the
dreadful move.

I snapped; my sister was leaving me for the
second time,
Especially during the phase when our
relationship reached its prime.
Nobody can take my three-leaf clover away, not
even them,
My next act is what I will never regret or
condemn.

"Why did you have to mention it, why are you
dumb?
Your words had made my entire body numb.
You forced me to pick that model and hit you on
your head,
and in front of my eyes, you bled out and were
dead."

The descriptive memory of her death makes me
sad,
Nevertheless, within seconds it made me glad.
My sister and I will now talk, share and laugh
forever,
and Kiara and Kabir can finally be together.

The truth is bitter, it will make one think I am
deranged,
With everyone leaving, I started feeling
estranged.

The only part of this activity confuses me,
anger turns into heavy sadness, and a smile so
meek.

SORRY, NAINA.

This one apology, I do not know how to make,
Naina is the one person whose anger I cannot
take.
How do I say it, should I be perfectly candid?
I had plenty of time to think, they were all
placid.

"Realistically, it is not my mistake, why should I
surrender?
Why did you keep calling me an offender?
You were always sweet to everyone, so why lash
out?

You trained me to receive everything but anger
throughout."

My eyes get teary whenever she shrieked at me,
They pinched my soul to the highest degree.
I love Naina, she is the muse for this drastic
decision,
Her death be so grisly, nobody dared to envision.

Kabir and Kiara dying gave me an exuberant
idea,
For the greater good, I decided to play with
Naina's phobia.
Took her hand, and she knew I had a surprise,
The plan was excellent, why did she despise?

I took her to see Kabir and Kiara, the now-fallen
To not catch her by surprise, I took the necessary
precaution.
Warned her, asked her not to jump and howl,
Not to get scared by the smell which was faintly
foul.

I suggested, since it was the best idea I ever had,
for her to stay back and none of us will ever be
sad.
I told her, that I now have Kabir and Kiara
onboard,

it was my error, I assumed Naina would
concord.

Frantically and with eyes of horror, she stepped
back;
I had no other choice but to yank and brutally
attack.
The loud bawling was going to out me very soon
had I not shut her mouth, we would break as a
commune.

The knife which cut my finger, when we were
cooking,
Was sitting right on the table, where Naina was
not looking.
A brief pause in her howling and kicking got me
dumbfounded,
she then accused me of being relentless, she
always felt hounded.

"I am going to the police, this is brutality,
What made you express your love with this
veracity?
Why did you do this, they are not your puppets,
Why did you think this idea will be celebrated
with trumpets?"

Naina was a smart woman, why did she say
something idiotic?

She made me self-reflect, I was being nothing
but neurotic.
I should not have done this, should not have
shown them,
My acts were a sacrifice for friendship, but a
decision she would condemn.

The idea was brilliant, I begged her and fell on
the floor,
I had to grab the knife that was placed next to
the door.
I sprinted, grabbed and then turned around to
look for her,
Within a minute, she decided to run and
disappear.

I heard her scream, something fell on her head,
When she tried to run away from friends that
were dead.
Luckily, she was with her friends, who eased her
in,
The knife then pierced through the front and the
back skin.

YOU CAN FORGIVE ME

Now that the truth is out; it is time to think.
Can we resolve this over wine glasses and clink?
My three-leaf clover is close to me, it is perfect,
I have an idea if nobody wants to object.

"How about we all move in together in a big
house,
others live in one room, and Naina becomes my
spouse.
We will cook, we will clean, we will divide all
chores,
I roll you up in suitcases, remote locations will
be our explorers."

With a little acceptance, see this moment as
triumphant.
We should celebrate this act of mine, a feeling so
jubilant!
I will cook for everyone, and make their
favourites for dinner,
And then we play card games, and dessert for
the winner.

This is exactly what we did if you remember
distinctly,
I had sworn to never talk to my clover; a
decision made strictly.
It was the day when we all had fought so severe,
Kabir and Kiara were in the room, barking at
each other.

Naina and I were on the balcony, gazing at the
stars,
we heard a sudden loud noise, we ashed out our
cigars.
Went running to see why was there a sound so
displeasing,
Kiara was sitting in the corner, while Kabir was
wheezing.

Soon enough, this had become a dramatic soap
opera,

The theme was always changing, there was a
wide range of genre.
We each took care of them, calmed them down
individually,
It was now time to wipe their tears, and listen to
them gradually.

They vented, they spoke and they cried out the
last tear,
They did not reveal the entire truth out of fear.
I knew something was different, something felt
strange,
The truth was to be known for the price of a
bitter exchange.

Badgering and pestering helped with my asking,
surprisingly
I went to talk to Naina, whose expression
changed drastically.
Kabir and Kiara were discussing the prospects
for Naina and me,
Then it would be all four in love, and not just
three.

This conversation struck a nerve, a fight broke
out,
The pitch of each voice was getting louder
throughout.
There came a point where everyone had fought,

Due to rejection, or even coming up with this
thought.

That is when we knew, it was time to take a
break,
nothing untoward could be said, a lot was at
stake.

So we bid adieu for the time we needed some
personal space,
A common mature consensus was decided upon
with such grace.

I believe, after a night of bitter rivalry and
temporary hate,
Being alone was magical, it took us only two
days to rejuvenate.
"My three-leaf clover, if we made it through this
travesty,
You can forgive me now, after all the confession
and honesty."

ANSWER ME

Wait, why is everyone making a face that angry?
Why is everyone staring at me so blankly?
Did they not forgive me, their face reckons such.
Without their words, I cannot understand much.

The one thing they did, was even bicker in their
sleep
now the trick they are using is downright cheap.
Why won't they answer me now, I need to be
forgiven,
Are they not seeing me in my miserable
condition?

"Do you want me to apologize again, I don't
mind.
Kiara, where is the soul that was always kind?

Kabir, will you not forgive your only true
friend?
Naina, isn't the empath inside you going to
mend?"

I panic, I get restless and I start to sweat,
I start to palpitate, and now my clothes are all
wet.
Should I go down on my knees and join my
hands tightly?
Do they want me to beg them like they're all
mighty?

I won't let them take charge of what they have
done,
Make them feel like they are the innocent one.
They have to take responsibility for what they
did;
Why is everything around here confusing and
turbid?

"Let us keep this simple now, shall we?
To articulate easily, you three owe me an
apology!
Did you really expect me to be mentally stable?
You decided to leave by saying something
fable!"

Silly me forgot that these numbskulls cannot
speak,
Their mouths are stitched shut; I need to make a
tweak.
I expect an apology, I might be a little paranoid
and maniacal,
Here is a lifeless bundle that I misunderstood as
paradisiacal.

Now is not the time to do this, I have some work
to do,
The act of keeping you near me needs to end
very soon.
I want to get the last thing done with, then it will
be just us
That is when your actions will be spoken of, and
in-depth, we will discuss.

THE LAST TASK TO BE DONE

After the discussion, I set the table for when I am back,
I have to complete the last work; I am not a hack.
This needs to be done properly, for I have promised,
I am someone who stands by his word, not someone dishonest.

So I pick the last bag of the remains, all mixed together,
Each body part had its own place, places where we gather.
I pick the last bag and sing the songs of a winner

Irrespective of anything now, I will always be a
ruthless sinner.

There is happiness in my whistle, a spring in my
step,
what feels like a pilgrimage, was once an
endless schlep.
I can do anything now; I know I am that capable.
I did kill three people to make our bond
unbreakable.
While marinating in my thoughts, I came to my
last destination,
It was the travel company from where we
booked our vacation.
I slowly entered the office, it was very late at
night,
Not a single bird chippered, not a single working
light.

The hearts were symbolic of the favourite
memory we cherish,
Each body part to where it belongs is a way for
me to replenish.
Replenish what was ours, leaving all our traces
behind,
The memories, the place and the intention, are
all intertwined.

I dropped the bag of hearts and started to dig
around,
There was a backyard where something lost was
never found.
I slowly dug a hole, opened the hearts and put
them there,
Except for one which I kept with me to be fair.

Naina's heart is what I will die with, it will get
buried with me,
it is going to be the wish that will set my
troubled soul free.
Having to die with the heart of a woman who
you always loved,
Naina was my muse, my happiness and I, her
beloved.

I walk back to the house, a feeling of serenity
just set in,
My steps were now elegant, the background
played some violin.
I see my house, and it shone brighter than before
Because it's just the three-leaf clover, the rest of
the world we ignore.

NEVER LETTING THEM GO AWAY

Falling in a circle surrounded by confessions of
frowns and follies,
we shared the experience of each other's last
tragedies.
My friends are complicated, yet so simple;
our minds were in perfect harmony, and now
nothing is nimble.

We form the three-leaf clover; I am never letting
them leave.
I finally have people who loved me enough to
believe.

I am going to lock them up in the sunniest of
hopeless days,
and in the times when I am drowning in despair.

Like the soft toys in my house, they have
become.
Balancing their weakened foam bodies with
strength I can fathom.
They will never be sunset causing any fleeting
moment of solace,
and the sunrise no longer forces me to en-garde
with a smiling face.
The days we recalled, like four friends never to
bid adieu.
While nobody is moving out for growth that is
no longer due.
We sat and shared the dismal days of the last,
since these were the bleak days of the amassed.

A harrowing memory, remember when our
fights broke out?
Kabir's birthday it was, celebrations were
exuberant and profound!
Everyone dressed up looked dreadful in black
and white;
dumb promises of separating were proclaimed
with no moral heights.

During the days of shared speeches and clinking
glasses of wine
we promised to stay close, never leave the other
person's side.
So, like the stem of the clover, I have decided to
stay;
holding my lucky leaves close, never letting
them go away.

www.ingramcontent.com/pod-product-compliance
Lightning Source LLC
LaVergne TN
LVHW050932200726
843508LV00011B/2327